Second April by Edna St Vincent Millay

Edna St. Vincent Millay was born on 22nd February 1892 in Rockland, Maine, the eldest of three daughters.

Her early years were tinted with much difficulty; divorced parents, poverty and a constant change of location.

Despite this once settled in Camden, Maine Edna developed her literary talents at a furious rate. By 15, she had published her poetry in the popular children's magazine St. Nicholas, the Camden Herald, and the high-profile anthology Current Literature.

In 1912, at 20, she entered her poem 'Renascence' in The Lyric Year poetry contest. Despite being considered the best poem it was only given fourth place. The ensuing uproar brought publicity and the offer of funding for her education at Vassar College. Here she wrote, both verse and plays as well as embarking on a series of affairs with women as she explored the wider world and all it offered.

Edna achieved significant fame when she won the Pulitzer Prize for Poetry in 1923 for 'The Ballad of the Harp-Weaver'. It was a magnificent triumph.

She married Eugen Jan Boissevain but on her wedding day she fell ill and he drove her to Manhattan for emergency surgery. He nursed her back to health with remarkable devotion. They were together, in an open marriage, until his death in 1949.

In the summer of 1936, Edna was riding in a station wagon when the door swung open and she was hurled into the pitch-darkness and rolled into a rocky gully. She survived but with severely damaged nerves in her spine and was to live the rest of her life in pain.

In 1942 in an article for The New York Times Magazine, Edna mourned the callous destruction of the Czechoslovak town of Lidice by Nazi forces in retaliation for the assassination of Reinhard Heydrich. The article would serve as the basis of her 32-page poem, 'Murder of Lidice' in 1942.

Edna St. Vincent Millay, after suffering a heart attack, fell down the stairs and died at her home on 1ᵗʰ October 1950. She was 58 years old.

Index of Contents

SPRING

To what purpose, April, do you return again?
Beauty is not enough.
You can no longer quiet me with the redness
Of little leaves opening stickily.
I know what I know.
The sun is hot on my neck as I observe
The spikes of the crocus.
The smell of the earth is good.
It is apparent that there is no death.
But what does that signify?
Not only under ground are the brains of men
Eaten by maggots,
Life in itself
Is nothing,
An empty cup, a flight of uncarpeted stairs.
It is not enough that yearly, down this hill,
April
Comes like an idiot, babbling and strewing flowers.

CITY TREES

The trees along this city street,
Save for the traffic and the trains,
Would make a sound as thin and sweet
As trees in country lanes.

And people standing in their shade
Out of a shower, undoubtedly
Would hear such music as is made
Upon a country tree.

Oh, little leaves that are so dumb
Against the shrieking city air,
I watch you when the wind has come,—
I know what sound is there.

THE BLUE-FLAG IN THE BOG

God had called us, and we came;
Our loved Earth to ashes left;
Heaven was a neighbor's house,
Open to us, bereft.

Gay the lights of Heaven showed,
And 'twas God who walked ahead;
Yet I wept along the road,
Wanting my own house instead.

Wept unseen, unheeded cried,
"All you things my eyes have kissed,
Fare you well! We meet no more,
Lovely, lovely tattered mist!

Weary wings that rise and fall
All day long above the fire!"—
Red with heat was every wall,
Rough with heat was every wire—

"Fare you well, you little winds
That the flying embers chase!
Fare you well, you shuddering day,
With your hands before your face!

And, ah, blackened by strange blight,
Or to a false sun unfurled,
Now forevermore goodbye,
All the gardens in the world!

On the windless hills of Heaven,
That I have no wish to see,
White, eternal lilies stand,
By a lake of ebony.

But the Earth forevermore
Is a place where nothing grows,—
Dawn will come, and no bud break;
Evening, and no blossom close.

Spring will come, and wander slow
Over an indifferent land,
Stand beside an empty creek,
Hold a dead seed in her hand."

God had called us, and we came,
But the blessed road I trod
Was a bitter road to me,
And at heart I questioned God.

"Though in Heaven," I said, "be all
That the heart would most desire,
Held Earth naught save souls of sinners
Worth the saving from a fire?

Withered grass,—the wasted growing!
Aimless ache of laden boughs!"
Little things God had forgotten
Called me, from my burning house.

"Though in Heaven," I said, "be all
That the eye could ask to see,
All the things I ever knew
Are this blaze in back of me."

"Though in Heaven," I said, "be all
That the ear could think to lack,
All the things I ever knew
Are this roaring at my back."

It was God who walked ahead,
Like a shepherd to the fold;
In his footsteps fared the weak,
And the weary and the old,

Glad enough of gladness over,
Ready for the peace to be,—
But a thing God had forgotten
Was the growing bones of me.

And I drew a bit apart,
And I lagged a bit behind,
And I thought on Peace Eternal,
Lest He look into my mind:

And I gazed upon the sky,
And I thought of Heavenly Rest,—

And I slipped away like water
Through the fingers of the blest!

All their eyes were fixed on Glory,
Not a glance brushed over me;
"Alleluia! Alleluia!"
Up the road,—and I was free.

And my heart rose like a freshet,
And it swept me on before,
Giddy as a whirling stick,
Till I felt the earth once more.

All the earth was charred and black,
Fire had swept from pole to pole;
And the bottom of the sea
Was as brittle as a bowl;

And the timbered mountain-top
Was as naked as a skull,—
Nothing left, nothing left,
Of the Earth so beautiful!

"Earth," I said, "how can I leave you?"
"You are all I have," I said;
"What is left to take my mind up,
Living always, and you dead?"

"Speak!" I said, "Oh, tell me something!
Make a sign that I can see!
For a keepsake! To keep always!
Quick!—before God misses me!"

And I listened for a voice;—
But my heart was all I heard;
Not a screech-owl, not a loon,
Not a tree-toad said a word.

And I waited for a sign;—
Coals and cinders, nothing more;
And a little cloud of smoke
Floating on a valley floor.

And I peered into the smoke
Till it rotted, like a fog:—
There, encompassed round by fire,
Stood a blue-flag in a bog!

Little flames came wading out,
Straining, straining towards its stem,
But it was so blue and tall
That it scorned to think of them!

Red and thirsty were their tongues,
As the tongues of wolves must be,
But it was so blue and tall—
Oh, I laughed, I cried, to see!

All my heart became a tear,
All my soul became a tower,
Never loved I anything
As I loved that tall blue flower!

It was all the little boats
That had ever sailed the sea,
It was all the little books
That had gone to school with me;

On its roots like iron claws
Rearing up so blue and tall,—
It was all the gallant Earth
With its back against a wall!

In a breath, ere I had breathed,—
Oh, I laughed, I cried, to see!—
I was kneeling at its side,
And it leaned its head on me!

Crumbling stones and sliding sand
Is the road to Heaven now;
Icy at my straining knees
Drags the awful under-tow;

Soon but stepping-stones of dust
Will the road to Heaven be,—
Father, Son and Holy Ghost,
Reach a hand and rescue me!

"There—there, my blue-flag flower;
Hush—hush—go to sleep;
That is only God you hear,
Counting up His folded sheep!

Lullabye—lullabye—
That is only God that calls,
Missing me, seeking me,

Ere the road to nothing falls!

He will set His mighty feet
Firmly on the sliding sand;
Like a little frightened bird
I will creep into His hand;

I will tell Him all my grief,
I will tell Him all my sin;
He will give me half His robe
For a cloak to wrap you in.

Lullabye—lullabye—"
Rocks the burnt-out planet free!—
Father, Son and Holy Ghost,
Reach a hand and rescue me!

Ah, the voice of love at last!
Lo, at last the face of light!
And the whole of His white robe
For a cloak against the night!

And upon my heart asleep
All the things I ever knew!—
"Holds Heaven not some cranny, Lord,
For a flower so tall and blue?"

All's well and all's well!
Gay the lights of Heaven show!
In some moist and Heavenly place
We will set it out to grow.

JOURNEY

Ah, could I lay me down in this long grass
And close my eyes, and let the quiet wind
Blow over me—I am so tired, so tired
Of passing pleasant places! All my life,
Following Care along the dusty road,
Have I looked back at loveliness and sighed;
Yet at my hand an unrelenting hand
Tugged ever, and I passed. All my life long
Over my shoulder have I looked at peace;
And now I fain would lie in this long grass
And close my eyes.
Yet onward!

Cat birds call
Through the long afternoon, and creeks at dusk
Are guttural. Whip-poor-wills wake and cry,
Drawing the twilight close about their throats.
Only my heart makes answer. Eager vines
Go up the rocks and wait; flushed apple-trees
Pause in their dance and break the ring for me;
Dim, shady wood-roads, redolent of fern
And bayberry, that through sweet bevies thread
Of round-faced roses, pink and petulant,
Look back and beckon ere they disappear.
Only my heart, only my heart responds.
Yet, ah, my path is sweet on either side
All through the dragging day,—sharp underfoot
And hot, and like dead mist the dry dust hangs—
But far, oh, far as passionate eye can reach,
And long, ah, long as rapturous eye can cling,
The world is mine: blue hill, still silver lake,
Broad field, bright flower, and the long white road
A gateless garden, and an open path:
My feet to follow, and my heart to hold.

EEL-GRASS

No matter what I say,
All that I really love
Is the rain that flattens on the bay,
And the eel-grass in the cove;
The jingle-shells that lie and bleach
At the tide-line, and the trace
Of higher tides along the beach:
Nothing in this place.

ELEGY BEFORE DEATH

There will be rose and rhododendron
When you are dead and under ground;
Still will be heard from white syringas
Heavy with bees, a sunny sound;

Still will the tamaracks be raining
After the rain has ceased, and still
Will there be robins in the stubble,
Brown sheep upon the warm green hill.

Spring will not ail nor autumn falter;
Nothing will know that you are gone,
Saving alone some sullen plough-land
None but yourself sets foot upon;

Saving the may-weed and the pig-weed
Nothing will know that you are dead,—
These, and perhaps a useless wagon
Standing beside some tumbled shed.

Oh, there will pass with your great passing
Little of beauty not your own,—
Only the light from common water,
Only the grace from simple stone!

THE BEAN-STALK

Ho, Giant! This is I!
I have built me a bean-stalk into your sky!
La,—but it's lovely, up so high!

This is how I came,—I put
Here my knee, there my foot,
Up and up, from shoot to shoot—
And the blessed bean-stalk thinning
Like the mischief all the time,
Till it took me rocking, spinning,
In a dizzy, sunny circle,
Making angles with the root,
Far and out above the cackle
Of the city I was born in,
Till the little dirty city
In the light so sheer and sunny
Shone as dazzling bright and pretty
As the money that you find
In a dream of finding money—
What a wind! What a morning!—

Till the tiny, shiny city,
When I shot a glance below,
Shaken with a giddy laughter,
Sick and blissfully afraid,
Was a dew-drop on a blade,
And a pair of moments after
Was the whirling guess I made,—

And the wind was like a whip

Cracking past my icy ears,
And my hair stood out behind,
And my eyes were full of tears,
Wide-open and cold,
More tears than they could hold,
The wind was blowing so,
And my teeth were in a row,
Dry and grinning,
And I felt my foot slip,
And I scratched the wind and whined,
And I clutched the stalk and jabbered,
With my eyes shut blind,—
What a wind! What a wind!

Your broad sky, Giant,
Is the shelf of a cupboard;
I make bean-stalks, I'm
A builder, like yourself,
But bean-stalks is my trade,
I couldn't make a shelf,
Don't know how they're made,
Now, a bean-stalk is more pliant—
La, what a climb!

WEEDS

White with daisies and red with sorrel
And empty, empty under the sky!—
Life is a quest and love a quarrel—
Here is a place for me to lie.

Daisies spring from damned seeds,
And this red fire that here I see
Is a worthless crop of crimson weeds,
Cursed by farmers thriftily.

But here, unhated for an hour,
The sorrel runs in ragged flame,
The daisy stands, a bastard flower,
Like flowers that bear an honest name.

And here a while, where no wind brings
The baying of a pack athirst,
May sleep the sleep of blessed things,

The blood too bright, the brow accurst.

PASSER MORTUUS EST

Death devours all lovely things;
Lesbia with her sparrow
Shares the darkness,—presently
Every bed is narrow.

Unremembered as old rain
Dries the sheer libation,
And the little petulant hand
Is an annotation.

After all, my erstwhile dear,
My no longer cherished,
Need we say it was not love,
Now that love is perished?

PASTORAL

If it were only still!—
With far away the shrill
Crying of a cock;
Or the shaken bell
From a cow's throat
Moving through the bushes;
Or the soft shock
Of wizened apples falling
From an old tree
In a forgotten orchard
Upon the hilly rock!

Oh, grey hill,
Where the grazing herd
Licks the purple blossom,
Crops the spiky weed!
Oh, stony pasture,
Where the tall mullein
Stands up so sturdy
On its little seed!

ASSAULT

I

I had forgotten how the frogs must sound
After a year of silence, else I think
I should not so have ventured forth alone
At dusk upon this unfrequented road.

II

I am waylaid by Beauty. Who will walk
Between me and the crying of the frogs?
Oh, savage Beauty, suffer me to pass,
That am a timid woman, on her way
From one house to another!

TRAVEL

The railroad track is miles away,
And the day is loud with voices speaking,
Yet there isn't a train goes by all day
But I hear its whistle shrieking.

All night there isn't a train goes by,
Though the night is still for sleep and dreaming
But I see its cinders red on the sky,
And hear its engine steaming.

My heart is warm with the friends I make,
And better friends I'll not be knowing,
Yet there isn't a train I wouldn't take,
No matter where it's going.

LOW-TIDE

These wet rocks where the tide has been,
Barnacled white and weeded brown
And slimed beneath to a beautiful green,
These wet rocks where the tide went down
Will show again when the tide is high
Faint and perilous, far from shore,
No place to dream, but a place to die,—

The bottom of the sea once more.
There was a child that wandered through
A giant's empty house all day,—
House full of wonderful things and new,
But no fit place for a child to play.

SONG OF A SECOND APRIL

April this year, not otherwise
Than April of a year ago,
Is full of whispers, full of sighs,
Of dazzling mud and dingy snow;
Hepaticas that pleased you so
Are here again, and butterflies.

There rings a hammering all day,
And shingles lie about the doors;
In orchards near and far away
The grey wood-pecker taps and bores;
The men are merry at their chores,
And children earnest at their play.

The larger streams run still and deep,
Noisy and swift the small brooks run
Among the mullein stalks the sheep
Go up the hillside in the sun,
Pensively,—only you are gone,
You that alone I cared to keep.

ROSEMARY

For the sake of some things
That be now no more
I will strew rushes
On my chamber-floor,
I will plant bergamot
At my kitchen-door.

For the sake of dim things
That were once so plain
I will set a barrel
Out to catch the rain,
I will hang an iron pot
On an iron crane.

Many things be dead and gone
That were brave and gay;
For the sake of these things
I will learn to say,
"An it please you, gentle sirs,"
"Alack!" and "Well-a-day!"

THE POET AND HIS BOOK

Down, you mongrel, Death!
Back into your kennel!
I have stolen breath
In a stalk of fennel!
You shall scratch and you shall whine
Many a night, and you shall worry
Many a bone, before you bury
One sweet bone of mine!

When shall I be dead?
When my flesh is withered,
And above my head
Yellow pollen gathered
All the empty afternoon?
When sweet lovers pause and wonder
Who am I that lie thereunder,
Hidden from the moon?

This my personal death?—
That lungs be failing
To inhale the breath
Others are exhaling?
This my subtle spirit's end?—
Ah, when the thawed winter splashes
Over these chance dust and ashes,
Weep not me, my friend!

Me, by no means dead
In that hour, but surely
When this book, unread,
Rots to earth obscurely,
And no more to any breast,
Close against the clamorous swelling
Of the thing there is no telling,
Are these pages pressed!

When this book is mould,
And a book of many
Waiting to be sold
For a casual penny,
In a little open case,
In a street unclean and cluttered,
Where a heavy mud is spattered
From the passing drays,

Stranger, pause and look;
From the dust of ages
Lift this little book,
Turn the tattered pages,
Read me, do not let me die!
Search the fading letters, finding
Steadfast in the broken binding
All that once was I!

When these veins are weeds,
When these hollowed sockets
Watch the rooty seeds
Bursting down like rockets,
And surmise the spring again,
Or, remote in that black cupboard,
Watch the pink worms writhing upward
At the smell of rain,

Boys and girls that lie
Whispering in the hedges,
Do not let me die,
Mix me with your pledges;
Boys and girls that slowly walk
In the woods, and weep, and quarrel,
Staring past the pink wild laurel,
Mix me with your talk,

Do not let me die!
Farmers at your raking,
When the sun is high,
While the hay is making,
When, along the stubble strewn,
Withering on their stalks uneaten,
Strawberries turn dark and sweeten
In the lapse of noon;

Shepherds on the hills,
In the pastures, drowsing
To the tinkling bells

Of the brown sheep browsing;
Sailors crying through the storm;
Scholars at your study; hunters
Lost amid the whirling winter's
Whiteness uniform;

Men that long for sleep;
Men that wake and revel;—
If an old song leap
To your senses' level
At such moments, may it be
Sometimes, though a moment only,
Some forgotten, quaint and homely
Vehicle of me!

Women at your toil,
Women at your leisure
Till the kettle boil,
Snatch of me your pleasure,
Where the broom-straw marks the leaf;
Women quiet with your weeping
Lest you wake a workman sleeping,
Mix me with your grief!

Boys and girls that steal
From the shocking laughter
Of the old, to kneel
By a dripping rafter
Under the discolored eaves,
Out of trunks with hingeless covers
Lifting tales of saints and lovers,
Travelers, goblins, thieves,

Suns that shine by night,
Mountains made from valleys,—
Bear me to the light,
Flat upon your bellies
By the webby window lie,
Where the little flies are crawling,—
Read me, margin me with scrawling,
Do not let me die!

Sexton, ply your trade!
In a shower of gravel
Stamp upon your spade!
Many a rose shall ravel,
Many a metal wreath shall rust
In the rain, and I go singing

Through the lots where you are flinging
Yellow clay on dust!

ALMS

My heart is what it was before,
A house where people come and go;
But it is winter with your love,
The sashes are beset with snow.

I light the lamp and lay the cloth,
I blow the coals to blaze again;
But it is winter with your love,
The frost is thick upon the pane.

I know a winter when it comes:
The leaves are listless on the boughs;
I watched your love a little while,
And brought my plants into the house.

I water them and turn them south,
I snap the dead brown from the stem;
But it is winter with your love,—
I only tend and water them.

There was a time I stood and watched
The small, ill-natured sparrows' fray;
I loved the beggar that I fed,
I cared for what he had to say,

I stood and watched him out of sight;
Today I reach around the door
And set a bowl upon the step;
My heart is what it was before,

But it is winter with your love;
I scatter crumbs upon the sill,
And close the window,—and the birds
May take or leave them, as they will.

INLAND

People that build their houses inland,
People that buy a plot of ground

Shaped like a house, and build a house there,
Far from the sea-board, far from the sound

Of water sucking the hollow ledges,
Tons of water striking the shore,—
What do they long for, as I long for
One salt smell of the sea once more?

People the waves have not awakened,
Spanking the boats at the harbor's head,
What do they long for, as I long for,—
Starting up in my inland bed,

Beating the narrow walls, and finding
Neither a window nor a door,
Screaming to God for death by drowning,—
One salt taste of the sea once more?

TO A POET THAT DIED YOUNG

Minstrel, what have you to do
With this man that, after you,
Sharing not your happy fate,
Sat as England's Laureate?
Vainly, in these iron days,
Strives the poet in your praise,
Minstrel, by whose singing side
Beauty walked, until you died.

Still, though none should hark again,
Drones the blue-fly in the pane,
Thickly crusts the blackest moss,
Blows the rose its musk across,
Floats the boat that is forgot
None the less to Camelot.

Many a bard's untimely death
Lends unto his verses breath;
Here's a song was never sung:
Growing old is dying young.
Minstrel, what is this to you:
That a man you never knew,
When your grave was far and green,
Sat and gossipped with a queen?

Thalia knows how rare a thing

Is it, to grow old and sing;
When a brown and tepid tide
Closes in on every side.
Who shall say if Shelley's gold
Had withstood it to grow old?

WRAITH

"Thin Rain, whom are you haunting,
That you haunt my door?"
—Surely it is not I she's wanting;
Someone living here before—
"Nobody's in the house but me:
You may come in if you like and see."

Thin as thread, with exquisite fingers,—
Have you seen her, any of you?—
Grey shawl, and leaning on the wind,
And the garden showing through?

Glimmering eyes,—and silent, mostly,
Sort of a whisper, sort of a purr,
Asking something, asking it over,
If you get a sound from her.—

Ever see her, any of you?—
Strangest thing I've ever known,—
Every night since I moved in,
And I came to be alone.

"Thin Rain, hush with your knocking!
You may not come in!
This is I that you hear rocking;
Nobody's with me, nor has been!"

Curious, how she tried the window,—
Odd, the way she tries the door,—
Wonder just what sort of people
Could have had this house before . . .

EBB

I know what my heart is like
Since your love died:

It is like a hollow ledge
Holding a little pool
Left there by the tide,
A little tepid pool,
Drying inward from the edge.

ELAINE

OH, come again to Astolat!
I will not ask you to be kind.
And you may go when you will go,
And I will stay behind.

I will not say how dear you are,
Or ask you if you hold me dear,
Or trouble you with things for you
The way I did last year.

So still the orchard, Lancelot,
So very still the lake shall be,
You could not guess—though you should guess—
What is become of me.

So wide shall be the garden-walk,
The garden-seat so very wide,
You needs must think—if you should think—
The lily maid had died.

Save that, a little way away,
I'd watch you for a little while,
To see you speak, the way you speak,
And smile,—if you should smile.

BURIAL

Mine is a body that should die at sea!
And have for a grave, instead of a grave
Six feet deep and the length of me,
All the water that is under the wave!

And terrible fishes to seize my flesh,
Such as a living man might fear,
And eat me while I am firm and fresh,—
Not wait till I've been dead for a year!

MARIPOSA

Butterflies are white and blue
In this field we wander through.
Suffer me to take your hand.
Death comes in a day or two.

All the things we ever knew
Will be ashes in that hour,
Mark the transient butterfly,
How he hangs upon the flower.

Suffer me to take your hand.
Suffer me to cherish you
Till the dawn is in the sky.
Whether I be false or true,
Death comes in a day or two.

THE LITTLE HILL

OH, here the air is sweet and still,
And soft's the grass to lie on;
And far away's the little hill
They took for Christ to die on.

And there's a hill across the brook,
And down the brook's another;
But, oh, the little hill they took,—
I think I am its mother!

The moon that saw Gethsemane,
I watch it rise and set:
It has so many things to see,
They help it to forget.

But little hills that sit at home
So many hundred years,
Remember Greece, remember Rome,
Remember Mary's tears.

And far away in Palestine,
Sadder than any other,
Grieves still the hill that I call mine,—

I think I am its mother!

DOUBT NO MORE THAT OBERON

Doubt no more that Oberon—
Never doubt that Pan
Lived, and played a reed, and ran
After nymphs in a dark forest,
In the merry, credulous days,—
Lived, and led a fairy band
Over the indulgent land!
Ah, for in this dourest, sorest
Age man's eye has looked upon,
Death to fauns and death to fays,
Still the dog-wood dares to raise—
Healthy tree, with trunk and root—
Ivory bowls that bear no fruit,
And the starlings and the jays—
Birds that cannot even sing—
Dare to come again in spring!

LAMENT

Listen, children:
Your father is dead.
From his old coats
I'll make you little jackets;
I'll make you little trousers
From his old pants.
There'll be in his pockets
Things he used to put there,
Keys and pennies
Covered with tobacco;
Dan shall have the pennies
To save in his bank;
Anne shall have the keys
To make a pretty noise with.
Life must go on,
And the dead be forgotten;
Life must go on,
Though good men die;
Anne, eat your breakfast;
Dan, take your medicine;
Life must go on;

I forget just why.

EXILED

Searching my heart for its true sorrow,
This is the thing I find to be:
That I am weary of words and people,
Sick of the city, wanting the sea;

Wanting the sticky, salty sweetness
Of the strong wind and shattered spray;
Wanting the loud sound and the soft sound
Of the big surf that breaks all day.

Always before about my dooryard,
Marking the reach of the winter sea,
Rooted in sand and dragging drift-wood,
Straggled the purple wild sweet-pea;

Always I climbed the wave at morning,
Shook the sand from my shoes at night,
That now am caught beneath great buildings,
Stricken with noise, confused with light.

If I could hear the green piles groaning
Under the windy wooden piers,
See once again the bobbing barrels,
And the black sticks that fence the weirs,

If I could see the weedy mussels
Crusting the wrecked and rotting hulls,
Hear once again the hungry crying
Overhead, of the wheeling gulls,

Feel once again the shanty straining
Under the turning of the tide,
Fear once again the rising freshet,
Dread the bell in the fog outside,—

I should be happy,—that was happy
All day long on the coast of Maine!
I have a need to hold and handle
Shells and anchors and ships again!

I should be happy, that am happy
Never at all since I came here.

I am too long away from water.
I have a need of water near.

THE DEATH OF AUTUMN

When reeds are dead and a straw to thatch the marshes,
And feathered pampas-grass rides into the wind
Like aged warriors westward, tragic, thinned
Of half their tribe, and over the flattened rushes,
Stripped of its secret, open, stark and bleak,
Blackens afar the half-forgotten creek,—
Then leans on me the weight of the year, and crushes
My heart. I know that Beauty must ail and die,
And will be born again,—but ah, to see
Beauty stiffened, staring up at the sky!
Oh, Autumn! Autumn!—What is the Spring to me?

ODE TO SILENCE

Aye, but she?
Your other sister and my other soul
Grave Silence, lovelier
Than the three loveliest maidens, what of her?
Clio, not you,
Not you, Calliope,
Nor all your wanton line,
Not Beauty's perfect self shall comfort me
For Silence once departed,
For her the cool-tongued, her the tranquil-hearted,
Whom evermore I follow wistfully,
Wandering Heaven and Earth and Hell and the four seasons through;
Thalia, not you,
Not you, Melpomene,
Not your incomparable feet, O thin Terpsichore,
I seek in this great hall,
But one more pale, more pensive, most beloved of you all.
I seek her from afar,
I come from temples where her altars are,
From groves that bear her name,
Noisy with stricken victims now and sacrificial flame,
And cymbals struck on high and strident faces
Obstreperous in her praise
They neither love nor know,
A goddess of gone days,

Departed long ago,
Abandoning the invaded shrines and fanes
Of her old sanctuary,
A deity obscure and legendary,
Of whom there now remains,
For sages to decipher and priests to garble,
Only and for a little while her letters wedged in marble,
Which even now, behold, the friendly mumbling rain erases,
And the inarticulate snow,
Leaving at last of her least signs and traces
None whatsoever, nor whither she is vanished from these places.
"She will love well," I said,
"If love be of that heart inhabiter,
The flowers of the dead;
The red anemone that with no sound
Moves in the wind, and from another wound
That sprang, the heavily-sweet blue hyacinth,
That blossoms underground,
And sallow poppies, will be dear to her.
And will not Silence know
In the black shade of what obsidian steep
Stiffens the white narcissus numb with sleep?
(Seed which Demeter's daughter bore from home,
Uptorn by desperate fingers long ago,
Reluctant even as she,
Undone Persephone,
And even as she set out again to grow
In twilight, in perdition's lean and inauspicious loam).
She will love well," I said,
"The flowers of the dead;
Where dark Persephone the winter round,
Uncomforted for home, uncomforted,
Lacking a sunny southern slope in northern Sicily,
With sullen pupils focussed on a dream,
Stares on the stagnant stream
That moats the unequivocable battlements of Hell,
There, there will she be found,
She that is Beauty veiled from men and Music in a swound."

"I long for Silence as they long for breath
Whose helpless nostrils drink the bitter sea;
What thing can be
So stout, what so redoubtable, in Death
What fury, what considerable rage, if only she,
Upon whose icy breast,
Unquestioned, uncaressed,
One time I lay,
And whom always I lack,

Even to this day,
Being by no means from that frigid bosom weaned away,
If only she therewith be given me back?"
I sought her down that dolorous labyrinth,
Wherein no shaft of sunlight ever fell,
And in among the bloodless everywhere
I sought her, but the air,
Breathed many times and spent,
Was fretful with a whispering discontent,
And questioning me, importuning me to tell
Some slightest tidings of the light of day they know no more,
Plucking my sleeve, the eager shades were with me where I went.
I paused at every grievous door,
And harked a moment, holding up my hand,—and for a space
A hush was on them, while they watched my face;
And then they fell a-whispering as before;
So that I smiled at them and left them, seeing she was not there.
I sought her, too,
Among the upper gods, although I knew
She was not like to be where feasting is,
Nor near to Heaven's lord,
Being a thing abhorred
And shunned of him, although a child of his,
(Not yours, not yours; to you she owes not breath,
Mother of Song, being sown of Zeus upon a dream of Death).
Fearing to pass unvisited some place
And later learn, too late, how all the while,
With her still face,
She had been standing there and seen me pass, without a smile,
I sought her even to the sagging board whereat
The stout immortals sat;
But such a laughter shook the mighty hall
No one could hear me say:
Had she been seen upon the Hill that day?
And no one knew at all
How long I stood, or when at last I sighed and went away.

There is a garden lying in a lull
Between the mountains and the mountainous sea,
I know not where, but which a dream diurnal
Paints on my lids a moment till the hull
Be lifted from the kernel
And Slumber fed to me.
Your foot-print is not there, Mnemosene,
Though it would seem a ruined place and after
Your lichenous heart, being full
Of broken columns, caryatides
Thrown to the earth and fallen forward on their jointless knees,

And urns funereal altered into dust
Minuter than the ashes of the dead,
And Psyche's lamp out of the earth up-thrust,
Dripping itself in marble wax on what was once the bed
Of Love, and his young body asleep, but now is dust instead.

There twists the bitter-sweet, the white wisteria
Fastens its fingers in the strangling wall,
And the wide crannies quicken with bright weeds;
There dumbly like a worm all day the still white orchid feeds;
But never an echo of your daughters' laughter
Is there, nor any sign of you at all
Swells fungous from the rotten bough, grey mother of Pieria!

Only her shadow once upon a stone
I saw,—and, lo, the shadow and the garden, too, were gone.

I tell you you have done her body an ill,
You chatterers, you noisy crew!
She is not anywhere!
I sought her in deep Hell;
And through the world as well;
I thought of Heaven and I sought her there;
Above nor under ground
Is Silence to be found,
That was the very warp and woof of you,
Lovely before your songs began and after they were through!
Oh, say if on this hill
Somewhere your sister's body lies in death,
So I may follow there, and make a wreath
Of my locked hands, that on her quiet breast
Shall lie till age has withered them!

(Ah, sweetly from the rest
I see
Turn and consider me
Compassionate Euterpe!)
"There is a gate beyond the gate of Death,
Beyond the gate of everlasting Life,
Beyond the gates of Heaven and Hell," she saith,
"Whereon but to believe is horror!
Whereon to meditate engendereth
Even in deathless spirits such as I
A tumult in the breath,
A chilling of the inexhaustible blood
Even in my veins that never will be dry,
And in the austere, divine monotony
That is my being, the madness of an unaccustomed mood.

This is her province whom you lack and seek;
And seek her not elsewhere.
Hell is a thoroughfare
For pilgrims,—Herakles,
And he that loved Euridice too well,
Have walked therein; and many more than these;
And witnessed the desire and the despair
Of souls that passed reluctantly and sicken for the air;
You, too, have entered Hell,
And issued thence; but thence whereof I speak
None has returned;—for thither fury brings
Only the driven ghosts of them that flee before all things.
Oblivion is the name of this abode: and she is there."

Oh, radiant Song! Oh, gracious Memory!
Be long upon this height
I shall not climb again!
I know the way you mean,—the little night,
And the long empty day,—never to see
Again the angry light,
Or hear the hungry noises cry my brain!
Ah, but she,
Your other sister and my other soul,
She shall again be mine;
And I shall drink her from a silver bowl,
A chilly thin green wine,
Not bitter to the taste,
Not sweet,
Not of your press, oh, restless, clamorous nine,—
To foam beneath the frantic hoofs of mirth—
But savoring faintly of the acid earth,
And trod by pensive feet
From perfect clusters ripened without haste
Out of the urgent heat
In some clear glimmering vaulted twilight under the odorous vine.

Lift up your lyres! Sing on!
But as for me, I seek your sister whither she is gone.

MEMORIAL TO D. C.

[VASSAR COLLEGE, 1918]

Oh, loveliest throat of all sweet throats,
Where now no more the music is,

With hands that wrote you little notes
I write you little elegies!

EPITAPH

Heap not on this mound
Roses that she loved so well;
Why bewilder her with roses,
That she cannot see or smell?
She is happy where she lies
With the dust upon her eyes.

PRAYER TO PERSEPHONE

Be to her, Persephone,
All the things I might not be;
Take her head upon your knee.
She that was so proud and wild,
Flippant, arrogant and free,
She that had no need of me,
Is a little lonely child
Lost in Hell,—Persephone,
Take her head upon your knee;
Say to her, "My dear, my dear,
It is not so dreadful here."

CHORUS

Give away her gowns,
Give away her shoes;
She has no more use
For her fragrant gowns;
Take them all down,
Blue, green, blue,
Lilac, pink, blue,
From their padded hangers;
She will dance no more
In her narrow shoes;
Sweep her narrow shoes
From the closet floor.

Let them bury your big eyes
In the secret earth securely,
Your thin fingers, and your fair,
Soft, indefinite-colored hair,—
All of these in some way, surely,
From the secret earth shall rise;
Not for these I sit and stare,
Broken and bereft completely;
Your young flesh that sat so neatly
On your little bones will sweetly
Blossom in the air.

But your voice,—never the rushing
Of a river underground,
Not the rising of the wind
In the trees before the rain,
Not the woodcock's watery call,
Not the note the white-throat utters,
Not the feet of children pushing
Yellow leaves along the gutters
In the blue and bitter fall,
Shall content my musing mind
For the beauty of that sound
That in no new way at all
Ever will be heard again.

Sweetly through the sappy stalk
Of the vigorous weed,
Holding all it held before,
Cherished by the faithful sun,
On and on eternally
Shall your altered fluid run,
Bud and bloom and go to seed;
But your singing days are done;
But the music of your talk
Never shall the chemistry
Of the secret earth restore.
All your lovely words are spoken.
Once the ivory box is broken,
Beats the golden bird no more.

DIRGE

Boys and girls that held her dear,
Do your weeping now;
All you loved of her lies here.

Brought to earth the arrogant brow,
And the withering tongue
Chastened; do your weeping now.

Sing whatever songs are sung,
Wind whatever wreath,
For a playmate perished young,

For a spirit spent in death.
Boys and girls that held her dear,
All you loved of her lies here.

SONNETS

I

We talk of taxes, and I call you friend;
Well, such you are,—but well enough we know
How thick about us root, how rankly grow
Those subtle weeds no man has need to tend,
That flourish through neglect, and soon must send
Perfume too sweet upon us and overthrow
Our steady senses; how such matters go
We are aware, and how such matters end.
Yet shall be told no meagre passion here;
With lovers such as we forevermore
Isolde drinks the draught, and Guinevere
Receives the Table's ruin through her door,
Francesca, with the loud surf at her ear,
Lets fall the colored book upon the floor.

II

Into the golden vessel of great song
Let us pour all our passion; breast to breast
Let other lovers lie, in love and rest;
Not we,—articulate, so, but with the tongue
Of all the world: the churning blood, the long
Shuddering quiet, the desperate hot palms pressed
Sharply together upon the escaping guest,
The common soul, unguarded, and grown strong.

Longing alone is singer to the lute;
Let still on nettles in the open sigh
The minstrel, that in slumber is as mute
As any man, and love be far and high,
That else forsakes the topmost branch, a fruit
Found on the ground by every passer-by.

III

Not with libations, but with shouts and laughter
We drenched the altars of Love's sacred grove,
Shaking to earth green fruits, impatient after
The launching of the colored moths of Love.
Love's proper myrtle and his mother's zone
We bound about our irreligious brows,
And fettered him with garlands of our own,
And spread a banquet in his frugal house.
Not yet the god has spoken; but I fear
Though we should break our bodies in his flame,
And pour our blood upon his altar, here
Henceforward is a grove without a name,
A pasture to the shaggy goats of Pan,
Whence flee forever a woman and a man.

IV

Only until this cigarette is ended,
A little moment at the end of all,
While on the floor the quiet ashes fall,
And in the firelight to a lance extended,
Bizarrely with the jazzing music blended,
The broken shadow dances on the wall,
I will permit my memory to recall
The vision of you, by all my dreams attended.
And then adieu,—farewell!—the dream is done.
Yours is a face of which I can forget
The color and the features, every one,
The words not ever, and the smiles not yet;
But in your day this moment is the sun
Upon a hill, after the sun has set.

V

Once more into my arid days like dew,
Like wind from an oasis, or the sound

Of cold sweet water bubbling underground,
A treacherous messenger, the thought of you
Comes to destroy me; once more I renew
Firm faith in your abundance, whom I found
Long since to be but just one other mound
Of sand, whereon no green thing ever grew.
And once again, and wiser in no wise,
I chase your colored phantom on the air,
And sob and curse and fall and weep and rise
And stumble pitifully on to where,
Miserable and lost, with stinging eyes,
Once more I clasp,—and there is nothing there.

VI

No rose that in a garden ever grew,
In Homer's or in Omar's or in mine,
Though buried under centuries of fine
Dead dust of roses, shut from sun and dew
Forever, and forever lost from view,
But must again in fragrance rich as wine
The grey aisles of the air incarnadine
When the old summers surge into a new.
Thus when I swear, "I love with all my heart,"
'Tis with the heart of Lilith that I swear,
'Tis with the love of Lesbia and Lucrece;
And thus as well my love must lose some part
Of what it is, had Helen been less fair,
Or perished young, or stayed at home in Greece.

VII

When I too long have looked upon your face,
Wherein for me a brightness unobscured
Save by the mists of brightness has its place,
And terrible beauty not to be endured,
I turn away reluctant from your light,
And stand irresolute, a mind undone,
A silly, dazzled thing deprived of sight
From having looked too long upon the sun.
Then is my daily life a narrow room
In which a little while, uncertainly,
Surrounded by impenetrable gloom,
Among familiar things grown strange to me
Making my way, I pause, and feel, and hark,
Till I become accustomed to the dark.

VIII

And you as well must die, beloved dust,
And all your beauty stand you in no stead;
This flawless, vital hand, this perfect head,
This body of flame and steel, before the gust
Of Death, or under his autumnal frost,
Shall be as any leaf, be no less dead
Than the first leaf that fell,—this wonder fled.
Altered, estranged, disintegrated, lost.
Nor shall my love avail you in your hour.
In spite of all my love, you will arise
Upon that day and wander down the air
Obscurely as the unattended flower,
It mattering not how beautiful you were,
Or how beloved above all else that dies.

IX

Let you not say of me when I am old,
In pretty worship of my withered hands
Forgetting who I am, and how the sands
Of such a life as mine run red and gold
Even to the ultimate sifting dust, "Behold,
Here walketh passionless age!"—for there expands
A curious superstition in these lands,
And by its leave some weightless tales are told.

In me no lenten wicks watch out the night;
I am the booth where Folly holds her fair;
Impious no less in ruin than in strength,
When I lie crumbled to the earth at length,
Let you not say, "Upon this reverend site
The righteous groaned and beat their breasts in prayer."

X

Oh, my beloved, have you thought of this:
How in the years to come unscrupulous Time,
More cruel than Death, will tear you from my kiss,
And make you old, and leave me in my prime?
How you and I, who scale together yet
A little while the sweet, immortal height
No pilgrim may remember or forget,

As sure as the world turns, some granite night
Shall lie awake and know the gracious flame
Gone out forever on the mutual stone;
And call to mind that on the day you came
I was a child, and you a hero grown?—
And the night pass, and the strange morning break
Upon our anguish for each other's sake!

XI

As to some lovely temple, tenantless
Long since, that once was sweet with shivering brass,
Knowing well its altars ruined and the grass
Grown up between the stones, yet from excess
Of grief hard driven, or great loneliness,
The worshiper returns, and those who pass
Marvel him crying on a name that was,—
So is it now with me in my distress.
Your body was a temple to Delight;
Cold are its ashes whence the breath is fled,
Yet here one time your spirit was wont to move;
Here might I hope to find you day or night,
And here I come to look for you, my love,
Even now, foolishly, knowing you are dead.

XII

Cherish you then the hope I shall forget
At length, my lord, Pieria?—put away
For your so passing sake, this mouth of clay
These mortal bones against my body set,
For all the puny fever and frail sweat
Of human love,—renounce for these, I say,
The Singing Mountain's memory, and betray
The silent lyre that hangs upon me yet?
Ah, but indeed, some day shall you awake,
Rather, from dreams of me, that at your side
So many nights, a lover and a bride,
But stern in my soul's chastity, have lain,
To walk the world forever for my sake,
And in each chamber find me gone again!

WILD SWANS

I looked in my heart while the wild swans went over.
And what did I see I had not seen before?
Only a question less or a question more;
Nothing to match the flight of wild birds flying.
Tiresome heart, forever living and dying,
House without air, I leave you and lock your door.
Wild swans, come over the town, come over
The town again, trailing your legs and crying!

Edna St Vincent Millay – A Short Biography

Edna St. Vincent Millay was born on 22nd February 1892 in Rockland, Maine, the eldest of three daughters.

When she was 12, in 1904, her parents divorced. Although they had already been separated for some years her mother, Cora, had found life raising three daughters with its domestic abuse and the haphazard finances of a relationship with their father, Henry, too difficult. The four of them now moved from town to town, enduring various illnesses and living in poverty. Despite their circumstances their mother insisted on travelling with a trunk full of classic literature. Their one indulgence was to be able to read Shakespeare, Milton and other literary greats.

Edna did manage to keep up a remote relationship with her father thorough letters they sent each other for several years.

She loved the outdoors. One of her prime sources for poetic inspiration was Nature with its seasons of life and death, growth and decay. She would spend hours alone immersed in its company throughout her life.

After some time Cora and her daughters settled in a small house at the property of Cora's aunt in Camden, Maine. Finally with a semblance stability around her Edna began to write poetry. Her literary journey had begun.

All of the sisters were independently minded, speaking frankly and rubbing up against authority. Edna had decided she wished to be known as 'Vincent'. Her school principal in a display of petty authority called her by any other name that started with a 'V'.

Edna developed her literary talents at a furious rate. She began by being published in the Camden High School literary magazine, The Megunticook. At 14 she won the St. Nicholas Gold Badge for poetry, and by 15, she had published her poetry in the popular children's magazine St. Nicholas, the Camden Herald, and the high-profile anthology Current Literature.

In 1912, at the age of 20, she entered her poem 'Renascence' in The Lyric Year poetry contest. Despite being considered the best poem it was only given fourth place. The ensuing uproar brought Edna a lot of publicity. The winner, Orrick Johns, stated that 'Renascence' was the best poem, and that the 'award was as much an embarrassment to me as a triumph.' Another prize winner offered her his $250 prize money. In its aftermath the wealthy arts patron Caroline B. Dow heard Edna reciting her poetry and playing piano at the Whitehall Inn in Camden, Maine, and was so impressed that she offered to pay for her education at Vassar College.

By 1913, somewhat later than would be usual (she was 21) she entered Vassar College. She was not fully prepared for its strict regimen. The college expected its students to be refined and live according to their status as young women. Edna by now enjoyed the more liberal social aspects of life including drinking, smoking and flirting. She managed to combine both, continuing to write verse and also several plays.

She liberally engaged in relationships including several with women. She was keen to explore and experience more of life.

This experience included trenchant views on society and how it saw and valued women. During the years of the Great War Edna was an ardent pacifist, but her views on war would later change in a very dramatic fashion.

Edna graduated in 1917 and left for New York. Her life here was openly bisexual. Edna described her life as 'very, very poor and very, very merry.' This was evidently enhanced by her own natural beauty and frivolous nature, although these were only a mask to a more serious woman who was writing powerful poetry.

To provide income she worked with the Provincetown Players on Macdougal Street and the Theatre Guild.

Edna began to use her poetry, as she became more deeply engaged in feminist activism, to explore those themes. She soon had no hesitation in writing on subjects others found taboo.

She also had a remarkable way of gathering relationships and keeping her partners intensely loyal to her, even after, in the case of two suitors who happened to be literary critics, rejecting their marriage proposals.

Her ability to fall in and out of love together with the sometimes cold and raw New York environment seemed to move her poetry into shorter, pithier poems which were published in many magazines including Vanity Fair and the Forum

In 1919, she wrote the anti-war play 'Aria da Capo', which starred her sister Norma Millay and which played at the Provincetown Playhouse in New York City.

The following year, 1920, Edna published 'A Few Figs From Thistles'. Its subject matter of female sexuality and feminism was immediately criticized by many. But her reputation was only growing.

In January 1921 Europe beckoned and Edna went to Paris, where she met and befriended the sculptors Thelma Wood and Constantin Brancusi, the photographer Man Ray, and had various affairs. She also became pregnant. Although a marriage license was obtained Edna instead returned to New England where her mother helped induce an abortion with alkanet, as recommended in her old copy of 'Culpeper's Complete Herbal'.

Edna achieved significant fame when she won the Pulitzer Prize for Poetry in 1923 for 'The Ballad of the Harp-Weaver'. It was a magnificent triumph. She was also the third woman in six years to win this very prestigious award, following in the footsteps of Sara Teasdale (1918) and Margaret Widdemer (1919).

At a house party in Croton-on-Hudson, New York she met Eugen Jan Boissevain, a Dutch-born coffee importer. He was the widower of the labor lawyer and war correspondent Inez Milholland, a political icon Edna had met during her Vassar years.

On their wedding day a few months later, Edna fell ill with intestinal problems. Eugen drove her to Manhattan for emergency surgery. Edna, referring to her Pulitzer Prize, quipped, 'If I die now, at least I'll be immortal.' He nursed her back to health with remarkable devotion. He was a self-proclaimed feminist and encouraged her to write whilst he took care of everything else. Their marriage was open, and both took several lovers during its course.

In 1924 along with several others she helped to found the Cherry Lane Theater and its remit of staging experimental drama.

A further source of revenue was from short stories she wrote for the mass-market magazine Ainslee's. With these she stayed under the radar. To protect her poetic identity with its smaller and more serious audience, she used a pseudonym; Nancy Boyd. The publisher eventually offered to double her fees if he could use her real name. She refused.

In 1925, for $9000 they purchased 345 acres of farm and outbuildings called Steepletop near Austerlitz, New York, which had once been a blueberry farm, and then added another 300 acres. From a Sears Roebuck catalog kit they built a barn, and followed this with a writing cabin and a tennis court. Edna even found the time to grow her own vegetables.

Several years later they purchased Ragged Island in Casco Bay, Maine, as a summer retreat. Edna frequently had problems with the servants they employed and despite her liberal tendencies and social inclusiveness wrote 'The only people I really hate are servants. They are not really human beings at all.'

In the summer of 1936, Edna was riding in a station wagon when the door suddenly swung open. She was hurled into the pitch-darkness and rolled into a rock-strewn gully. She survived but with severely damaged nerves in her spine which required frequent surgeries and hospitalizations and at least daily doses of morphine. Edna was to live the rest of her life in pain.

By 1940 she was sufficiently alarmed by the rise of fascism to advocate for the U.S. to enter the war against the Axis powers. She later worked with the Writers' War Board and published a book of propaganda poems, 'Make Bright the Arrows: A 1940s Notebook', which managed to alienate even her most appreciative critics.

In 1942 in an article for The New York Times Magazine, Edna mourned the callous destruction of the Czechoslovak town of Lidice. Nazi forces had razed it to the ground, slaughtered its male inhabitants and scattered its surviving residents in retaliation for the assassination of Reinhard Heydrich. The article would serve as the basis of her 32-page poem, 'Murder of Lidice' in 1942.

In 1943, Edna was the sixth person and the second woman to be awarded the Frost Medal for her lifetime contribution to American poetry.

Despite the excellent sales of her books in the 1930s, her declining reputation, constant medical bills, and increasingly frequent demands from her mentally-ill sister Kathleen, meant that for most of her last years Edna was in debt to her publisher.

She did however quietly purchase a racing stable to indulge her passion for thoroughbred horse-racing. It would absorb much of her remaining income.

In 1949 after a twenty-six year marriage Boissevain died after a battle with lung cancer. Edna lived alone for the last year of her life. She drank heavily and lived almost as a recluse.

Edna St. Vincent Millay, after suffering a heart attack, fell down the stairs and died at her home on 19th October 1950. She was found approximately eight hours after her death. She was 58 years old.

She is buried alongside her husband at Steepletop, Austerlitz, New York.

Edna St Vincent Millay – A Concise Bibliography

Poems

Renascence & Other Poems (1917)
A Few Figs From Thistles: Poems & Four Sonnets (1920)
Second April (1921)
The Ballad of the Harp-Weaver (1922)
Poems (1923)
Distressing Dialogues, preface by Edna St. Vincent Millay (written as pseudonym Nancy Boyd) (1924)
The Buck in the Snow & Other Poems (1928)
Fatal Interview (Sonnets) (1931)
Wine from These Grapes (1934)
Conversation at Midnight (Narrative poem) (1937)
Huntsman, What Quarry? (1939)
There Are No Islands, Any More: Lines Written in Passion and in Deep Concern for England, France, and My Own Country (1940)
Make Bright the Arrows: 1940 Notebook (Poems) (1940)
The Murder of Lidice (Poem) (1942)
Second April and The Buck in the Snow, introduction by William Rose Benét (1950)
Mine the Harvest (Poems) (Edited by Norma Millay) (1954)

Translator

Flowers of Evil by Charles Baudelaire (with George Dillon) (1936)

Plays

Aria da capo (one-act play in verse; first produced in Greenwich Village, NY, December 5, 1919) (Also directed) (1921)
The Lamp and the Bell (Five-act play; first produced June 18, 1921)
Two Slatterns and a King: A Moral Interlude (1921)
Three Plays (Two Slatterns and a King, Aria da Capo, and The Lamp and the Bell) (1926)
The Princess Marries the Page (one-act play) (1932)

Opera

The King's Henchman (three-act play; New York, February 17, 1927) (Librettist)

Letters

Letters of Edna St. Vincent Millay (Edited by Allan Ross Macdougall) (1952)

www.ingramcontent.com/pod-product-compliance
Lightning Source LLC
Chambersburg PA
CBHW021946040426
42448CB00008B/1256